DISCOVER THROUGH
CRAFT

RECYCLING & REUSING

By Louise Spilsbury

W
FRANKLIN WATTS
LONDON•SYDNEY

Franklin Watts
Published in Great Britain in 2017 by
The Watts Publishing Group

Copyright © Franklin Watts 2014
All rights reserved.

Series editor: Amy Stephenson
Series designer: Jeni Child
Crafts: Rita Storey
Craft photography: Tudor Photography
Picture researcher: Diana Morris

Picture credits:
Kostiantyn Ablazor/Shutterstock: 23br. AGL Productions istockphoto:
19b. Atelier/Shutterstock: 26t. atm2003 Shutterstock: 6-7 bg. bibiphoto
Shutterstock: 31. Stephane Bidouse Shutterstock: 12b. bikeriderlondon/
Shutterstock: 16b Maxim Blinkov/Shutterstock: 19t. Joerg Boething/Alamy:
22. Nicole Cioe/istockphoto: 11bl. Graham Corney/Alamy: 27b. cozyta/
Shutterstock: 5t. craftvisions/istockphoto: 7b. Dmstudio/Dreamstime: 6t.
gabriel12/Shutterstock: 5b. gubgils/Shutterstock: 5c. kao/Shutterstock:
14-15bg. keafttikorn/Shutterstock: 18-19bg. Kietr/Shutterstock: 6b. Dmitri
Kisilev/Dreamstime: 18tl. Gaby Koojiman/Dreamstime: 18cl. Rusian
Kudrin/Shutterstock: 19c. Richard Lammerts/Dreamstime: 8t. Jon Le-Bon/
Shutterstock: 30. Marjanneke/Dreamstime: 28t. Ingrid Masik/Shutterstock:
10t. Dieter Meyrl/istockphoto: 16t. Oleg Mikhaylor/Shutterstock: 27t.Pejan
Mikikovic/Shutterstock: 26-27b/g. Monticello/Shutterstock: 7t. Jeff Morgan/
Alamy: 20t. msk.nina/istockphoto: 28b. 97/istockphoto: 14b. paimaria/
Shutterstock: 4. Pashabo/Shutterstock: front cover logo. photographe.eu/
Shutterstock: 11br. Hugette Rose/Shutterstock: 8c. Olivia Kaufman-Rovira:
20b. Dario Sabljak/Shutterstock: 22-23bg. Mark Schwettmann/Shutterstock:
15t sizov/Shutterstock: 10-11 bg. Anton Starikov/Dreamstime: 18tr. Piti Tan/
Shutterstock: 8b. Tchara/Shutterstock: front cover main. Richard Thomas/
Dreamstime: 1. Toa55/Shutterstock: 24t. totophoto/Shutterstock: 12t.
Vvoevale/Dreamstime: 18cr. S P Widoff/Shutterstock: 32. Ivonne Wierink/
Dreamstime: 16c. Kathy de Witt/Alamy: 24b. Worradirek/Shutterstock: 15b.

Every attempt has been made to clear copyright. Should there be any
inadvertent omission please apply to the publisher for rectification.

Dewey number: 363.7'282
ISBN: 978 1 4451 5488 6

Printed in China

Franklin Watts
An imprint of Hachette Children's Group
Part of The Watts Publishing Group
Carmelite House
50 Victoria Embankment
London EC4Y 0DZ
An Hachette UK company
www.hachette.co.uk
www.franklinwatts.co.uk

FSC
MIX
Paper from
responsible sources
FSC® C104740

CONTENTS

LIVE
BORDERS

Words in **bold** can be found in the glossary on page 30.

Some of the projects in this book require scissors, paint, tin cans and glue. We would recommend that children are supervised by a responsible adult when using these things and must always wear gloves if handling compost.

REUSING AND RECYCLING

**The waste we make can cause problems.
Reusing, recycling and reducing can help solve the problems.**

Rubbish dumps

How many of the things you use every day do you throw in the bin? In the UK, 82,000 tonnes of rubbish is thrown away every day! Where do you think the waste goes? Rubbish trucks take some waste to **landfill** sites or **incinerators**. Landfill waste is dumped in deep holes or on top of the ground. Incinerators burn other rubbish. Some waste stays in landfill for hundreds or thousands of years. Also, as the waste rots it can **pollute** soil and water.

TIP: One of the best ways to make less waste is by **reducing** how much stuff you buy. Try only buying the things you need to reduce your waste.

The packets, paper, bottles and other stuff people throw away ends up in landfill sites like this.

Wasting energy and raw materials

Making new things uses a lot of **energy**. Factories use a lot of electricity to run the machines that make the things we use. Lorries and ships use fuel to carry **raw materials** to the factories and **goods** from the factories to shops. When fuels such as oil or coal are burned to generate energy, this releases gases into the **atmosphere** that cause **global warming**.

Many power stations burn fossil fuels such as oil and gas. Factories use a lot of power to make things.

How reusing and recycling help

Reusing is when we use something again. Recycling is when we use waste to make something new. When we reuse and recycle, landfill space is saved and there is less pollution. Recycling saves electricity and fuel, too. Reusing is even better than recycling because it often doesn't use any extra energy.

Products with this symbol can be recycled.

Glass bottles are easy to recycle. Special bottle banks are used to collect lots of glass, before it is taken away to be recycled.

Quick FACTS

- The UK throws away 82,000 tonnes of rubbish every day.
- Some waste is burned in incinerators.
- Making new things uses lots of energy.

PAPER

Most types of paper are made using fibres of wood from trees.

How is paper made?

To make paper, first a tree is cut down. Its bark is peeled off and the wood is chopped into small pieces. These pieces are boiled with water and chemicals to make a slushy pulp. The pulp is poured onto a fine wire mesh that lets the water drain out of it. Then the mat of wet **fibres** left behind is pressed between rollers and dried to form paper.

HAVE A GO
Collect all the paper that your class or family recycles in a week. Put it in boxes for recycling. Work out how many boxes of paper you will recycle in a month and in a year. How could you reduce your paper usage?

These logs will be taken to a paper factory.

Waste paper

Paper is very useful, but making paper can cause problems, too. Paper mills use huge amounts of energy and use more water than any other type of factory. Waste from paper mills can pollute water and soil. Paper that is thrown away, instead of being reused or recycled, takes up lots of space in landfill sites.

Stacks of paper are thrown away every day. How much of the paper you use is recycled? Could you reuse some of it?

Waste paper can be made into lots of interesting things, such as plates, baskets or even decorations, like this paper bird.

Saving paper

There are lots of things you can do to reduce paper waste. You could buy second-hand books, use the library or share magazines with friends. Buy recycled paper and use the back of waste paper to make notes. You can also send greeting cards by email and reuse cards by making them into gift tags!

? How does recycling paper help the environment? Turn the page to find out.

How recycling helps

Recycling waste paper into new paper products saves water, energy, landfill space and trees! Making recycled paper saves up to 70 per cent of the energy needed to make new paper. Less energy means that less **greenhouse gas** is produced. A tonne of paper made from recycled paper also saves up to 17 trees and uses half the amount of water used to make non-recycled paper.

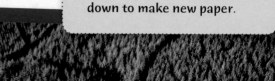

Huge areas of forest are cut down to make new paper.

Paper is squashed into blocks ready for recycling.

These stacks of recycled cardboard are ready to be made into new boxes.

QUIZ TIME!

When large areas of forest are cut down we call this:

a. timber

b. deforestation

c. clearing

Answer on page 32.

Quick FACTS

- Most paper is made from pulped wood.
- Recycled paper uses much less energy and water than it takes to make new paper.
- Recycling paper saves trees.

Make this

You can help wildlife by recycling and reusing, too. Make a bird feeder from an old juice or milk carton to attract wild birds to your school or garden.

You could keep a record of the birds that visit your feeder. Remember to keep it topped up with seeds.

2
Tear up lots of small pieces of scrap tissue paper. Cover the carton by pasting overlapping layers of tissue paper onto it with glue. Leave to dry.

3
Decorate the carton by gluing on leaves or twigs. To make perches, push two pencils through the bottom of the carton, one just above the other.

! Ask an adult to help you push the pencils through and make a hole in the top.

1 Cut a large rectangle from the side of your carton, about 5 cm from the bottom of the carton.

4
Make a hole in the top and thread some string through. Fill the bottom of the feeder with bird seed. Hang up your bird feeder outside.

GLASS

**Glass is used to make many things.
It is also easy to reuse and recycle.**

Glass can be made into lots of different shapes and in many different colours.

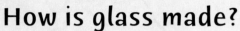

How is glass made?

Glass is made by melting together sand, **soda ash** and **lime** in an incredibly hot **furnace**. Melted glass is a hot liquid. It is shaped by people or machines to make bottles, glasses, windows and many other things. Special sand, called silica, is used to make clear glass. Other materials are added to make different colours and other types of glass. Glass is a perfect material for storing food or drink because it doesn't affect its taste.

Reuse and recycle glass

It's easy to reuse and recycle glass. We can reuse glass jars as small containers and we can use bottles as vases for flowers. When glass is recycled it is sorted by colour and then washed. Then it is crushed, melted and moulded into new products such as glassware and jewellery.

Problems with glass

To get the materials needed to make glass, such as sand and the limestone rock to make lime, people dig huge holes called quarries. They destroy the **habitats** of lots of animals, birds and other wildlife that live in the area because very few trees or plants can grow in quarries. Glass that ends up in landfill sites will take one million years to break down.

There are lots of clever ways to reuse glass. Here, bits of coloured glass have been used to decorate a wall.

You should wash glass bottles and jars before you recycle or reuse them.

? What can we save if we recycle, rather than make new glass? Turn the page to find out.

Glass is a perfect material for recycling. It can be recycled into new glass containers again and again and again.

How recycling helps

Recycling glass saves raw materials and money. Recycled glass melts at a lower temperature than raw materials so it uses less energy, too. The energy saved by recycling just one bottle could run a computer for 30 minutes! Using less energy also reduces the amount of greenhouse gases released into the atmosphere. Recycling glass also means no new land is dug up for sand or lime.

QUIZ TIME!

Glass is usually separated into different colours before recycling. Is it because…

a. **glass keeps its colour after recycling**

b. **only certain colours of glass can be recycled**

c. **people like colour coding their bottles and jars?**

Answer on page 32.

Quick *FACTS*

- Glass is made by melting sand and other raw materials.
- It is perfect for storing food and drink.
- Glass can be recycled again and again.

The walls, floor and pillars of this building are all made from old glass bottles!

Make this

Reuse an empty glass bottle or jar by turning it into a colourful vase.

You could make a desk tidy for pens and pencils. What other types of storage container could you make?

3 Use glue to paste the circles onto the outside of a bottle or jar. Overlap the circles to make a patten.

1 Draw around a jar lid or other round object many times onto coloured tissue paper.

2 Cut out the tissue paper circles.

4 Decorate with glitter glue and leave to dry. Put some water in your vase and add some flowers.

METALS

The metals we use the most are steel and aluminium. What do you think we use them for?

Metals at home

Steel is very strong and lightweight. Many cans that hold things such as food, toiletries and paint are made of steel. Steel is also used in bottle tops and jar lids. Aluminium is more **flexible**. It can be rolled so it is very thin. We use it to make cans for food and drinks, food trays and yoghurt pot lids. Aluminium is also made into foil for cooking and wrapping up food.

Next time you go to a supermarket, think about how many different items are sold in metal tins.

Where do metals come from?

Aluminium and steel are made from materials in rocks. Digging up these rocks is called **mining**. Aluminium is found in a rock called bauxite. After aluminium is taken from the rock, it is heated with other chemicals and has electricity passed through it. This uses a lot of energy. Steel is made from **iron ore** and limestone. The iron ore and limestone are heated to a very high temperature to make liquid steel. The liquid is poured into moulds. When it cools down the steel hardens into the shape of the mould.

Mines like this can damage the land and stop plants and animals living there.

HAVE A GO

Steel is magnetic, and aluminium is not. Use a **magnet** to see if you can pick up paper clips. Now put the magnet against an empty drinks can. Does the magnet pull towards it? Which items do you think are steel and which are aluminium?

How are metals recycled?

Aluminium and steel can be separated using a magnet. Aluminium items are crushed, chopped into pieces and melted. The liquid metal is cooled and rolled into thin sheets to make new aluminium things, such as cans. Steel is melted together with more iron ore and limestone. The liquid metal is cooled in a mould and cut into blocks. These are cut or melted again to make new steel things.

Giant magnets are used to pick up steel waste.

? How much energy does recycling cans save? Turn the page to find out.

How recycling helps

It takes as much energy to make a single new can as it does to recycle 20 used cans, so recycling metal saves energy. It can take over 100 years for an aluminium can to break down, so recycling cans will save space in landfill sites. Recycling also means less land is dug up for mines and stops dust and waste from new mines polluting water and soil.

Fish and other wildlife can die in rivers polluted by waste from mines.

Metal cans can be reused to make all kinds of things, such as this amazing toy car!

Quick *FACTS*

- Metals make good packaging.
- Materials that make metals are mined from the ground.
- Steel is magnetic and aluminuim is not.
- Magnets help us to recycle metals.

QUIZ TIME!

Recycling just one aluminium can save enough energy to run a television for how long?

a. 3 minutes

b. 3 hours

c. 3 days

Answer on page 32.

Make this

Empty tin cans, nuts and bolts and a metal scourer can be reused and made into a fun tin can man.

1 Ask an adult to glue a small tin can on top of a larger tin can. (Glue the open ends together.)

! This activity needs strong glue or a glue gun. Ask an adult to help you. Make sure you also ask permission before using any of these items.

2 Glue a metal scourer on top of the small can to make hair. Pull out some of the strands to give your tin man crazy hair.

3 Glue an old teaspoon on for a nose.

You could make several tin can people and then act out a story with them about recycling and reusing.

4 Glue on other bits of metal such as nuts, bolts, washers and rings for eyes and arms.

17

PLASTICS

Plastic is one of the most widely used materials in the world. How can we reuse and recycle it?

Plastic is used to make many of the things we use every day.

What is plastic?

Plastic is a material that is usually made from oil. It is used to make toys, furniture and many other things. Plastic is useful because it can be made to be light or heavy, strong or weak and it is waterproof. It can be clear or coloured and can be moulded into millions of different shapes. Lots of packaging is made from plastic, such as drinks bottles.

QUIZ TIME!

How many years does it take a plastic bottle to rot away in a landfill site?

a. 5 months

b. 50 years

c. around 500 years

Answer on page 32.

Problems with plastic

Because most plastic is made from oil it is not **biodegradable**. Some plastic waste is burnt in incinerators. Smoke from the incinerators causes air pollution. Other plastic waste can end up in the ocean. Animals that get tangled in plastic waste can drown. The ocean can also break plastic into tiny pieces. If animals swallow these pieces they can get sick or even die. Because of this, new types of plastic are now being made from materials that are biodegradable.

This turtle has died because it became tangled in plastic waste. It may have drowned or not been able to swim to catch its food.

How does recycling help?

It takes about 25 recycled plastic bottles to make one fleece jacket.

Recycling plastic reduces waste and litter, saves oil and energy and reduces pollution. Old plastic bottles can be made into T-shirts, fleece jackets, kayaks, chairs, carpets and other things. Plastic bags can be recycled into new plastic bags. But it is always better to reuse plastic if you can.

Oil rigs drill for oil, which is used to make plastic. We need to recycle plastic because supplies of oil will not last forever.

? How do you think plastic is recycled? Turn the page to find out.

How plastic is recycled

At a recycling plant, plastic waste is sorted into different types. Then it is pressed and squashed into big blocks. These blocks are chopped and shredded into small flakes or pellets. The pellets are washed and dried. Then they are melted down to make hot, liquid plastic. This is poured into moulds to form new objects when it cools and hardens again.

Melted plastic poured into this mould has cooled and hardened into the shape of a new toy.

There are other ways to reduce plastic waste. You can buy reusable plastic drinks bottles or use old plastic bottles to make something new, like a raft!

Quick FACTS

- Most plastic is made from oil.
- It can be hard or soft and moulded into all kinds of shapes.
- Plastic takes a long time to break down and can harm wildlife.

 HAVE A GO Do a survey of the plastic items your family uses. How many plastic things are in your bedroom and kitchen? How many things come in plastic packets? How do you think you can reduce the amount of plastic you use?

Make this

You can reuse and recycle all kinds of household waste in fun ways. Plastic drinks bottles are easy to turn into musical shakers.

To make shakers with different sounds, you could try using dry rice, lentils, beans or sand instead of pasta.

1 Put a handful of dry pasta shapes into a clean and dry plastic drinks bottle. Screw on the lid tightly.

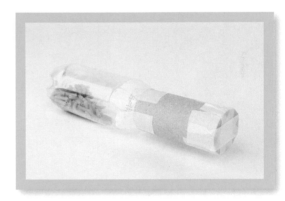

2 Place a cardboard tube over the neck of the bottle and tape it in place. Tape over the open end of the tube.

3 Tear up lots of small pieces of tissue paper. Use glue to paste layers of tissue paper onto the bottle and tube. Leave to dry.

4 Decorate the shaker with paint and leave to dry. You could make a second shaker for a friend.

CLOTHES AND TEXTILES

Did you know that you can reuse and recycle clothes and textiles in different ways, too?

Cotton picked from cotton plants in India can travel thousands of kilometres before it is made into clothes and sold in shops around the world.

How are textiles made?

Most clothes and textiles are made from cotton, **polyester** or a mixture of both. Cotton is a **natural** material that comes from the cotton plant. It is grown in hot countries, such as India. Polyester is a **synthetic** material that is made from oil. Machines in huge factories turn the materials into textiles by **weaving** them into big sheets of fabric.

Problems with clothing waste

In the UK more than one million tonnes of clothes are thrown away every year. When clothes and textiles are thrown away, all of the water, energy and materials used to make them are wasted. Plastic-based fabrics, such as polyester, do not biodegrade easily and can build up in landfill sites. Rain can wash out dyes and chemicals from the clothes, which pollute rivers and land.

HAVE A GO
Why not have a clothes swapping day at school or with friends. You could all bring along clothes you or your family don't wear anymore and swap them for other clothes.

Reusing clothes and textiles

People reuse clothes and textiles in different ways. You can mend fabrics when they get damaged instead of throwing them away. You can also give used clothes and textiles to charity shops so someone else can buy them. And you could buy your own clothes from a charity shop, too! In some places unwanted clothes are put in recycling bins. They are then collected and given to people who need extra clothing.

You could mend a hole in old clothes by covering it with a colourful patch.

Buying second-hand clothes is cheap, fun – and it helps the planet!

? What happens to clothes that are recycled? Turn the page to find out.

Old textiles can be cut up and turned into new things, like these colourful stuffed elephants.

QUIZ TIME!

Some farmers put chemicals on their fields to help plants (such as cotton) grow. What are these called?

a. pesticides
b. food
c. fertilisers

Answer on page 32.

How textiles are recycled

Clothes and textiles can be recycled, too. Old cotton clothes that are worn out can be shredded into fibres. These are blended together, spun into threads and made into new fabric. Old textiles can be cut up and sewn together again to make new items, like turning a curtain into a dress or a cushion cover. Scraps of fabric can also be made into patchwork blankets, or even toys.

Quick FACTS

• Cotton comes from the cotton plant, which is grown in hot countries.
• In the UK over one million tonnes of clothes are thrown away every year.
• Textiles are shredded into fibres when they are recycled.

Bags of clothes waiting to be recycled.

Make this

Reusing the pocket from an old pair of jeans means this crafty notebook will always have your pens and pencils to hand.

! Make sure you ask permission before you cut up any old clothes.

What other things could you add a pocket to? By adding lots of pockets to a strip of fabric you could make a storage system for your room.

1 Cut a pocket from an old pair of jeans. Be careful not to cut through the stitching that holds the pocket together.

2 Cut a strip of denim about 4 cm wide. It should be as long as your notebook and have a seam running down the middle.

3 Glue the strip of denim down both the front and back sides of your notebook. It should wrap around the spine.

4 Glue your pocket onto the front of your notebook. Decorate the notebook with stick-on shapes, sequins or jewels. Fill the pouch with pens, pencils and other tools.

WHAT IS COMPOSTING?

Composting is a way of recycling kitchen and garden waste.

Food and garden waste make up nearly half of all the rubbish that is thrown away.

Why is compost important?

Every year people throw away millions of tonnes of food and garden waste. This includes things like fruit and vegetable peelings, tea bags, grass cuttings and dead leaves. When large amounts of this waste rots in a landfill site it releases **methane**. Methane is a greenhouse gas that contributes to global warming. Composting is one way to reduce how our waste harms the planet.

QUIZ TIME!

Why do you think it is not a good idea to put fish, meat, dairy or oily food into your compost bin? Is it because...

a. it will make your compost smelly

b. compost worms don't like it

c. it will attract mice and rats?

Answer on page 32.

What is compost?

Digging compost into the soil means plants get nutrients to help them grow.

Compost is nature's way of recycling! Food and garden waste is biodegradable. It will **decompose** easily. When food and garden waste has rotted down for a long time, it turns into compost. Compost is a crumbly, soil-like material that is full of **nutrients**. People spread it on fields and gardens so the nutrients help new plants to grow.

How does composting work?

Decomposers are living things that break down waste to make compost. Some decomposers are animals we can see, such as worms, snails and flies. Other decomposers, such as **bacteria**, are **micro-organisms**. These are so tiny we can only see them with a microscope. Micro-organisms do most of the decomposition work, eating and **digesting** the waste, which turns it into compost.

It takes several months for decomposers to turn waste into compost.

? How easy do you think it is to make your own compost? Turn the page to find out.

How to make compost

You can buy a compost bin for your garden or make one from wood, bricks, wire or a metal drum. Put in a mix of dry stuff, such as dry leaves and twigs and damp stuff, such as food scraps and tea bags (but not meat, fish, dairy products or oily food). Decomposing needs air too, so make sure there are holes in the bin so air flows through it.

Compost is ready to dig into your garden when the mixture turns dark and crumbly, looks like soil and smells sweet.

TIP: You should always wear gloves when you touch compost and wash your hands afterwards.

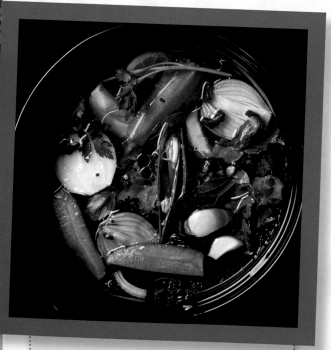

Don't worry if you haven't got room for a compost bin. Another way to cut down on your food waste is by making soup with your leftovers.

Quick FACTS

• Half of the rubbish people throw away is food and garden waste.
• Worms, snails and flies are all decomposers that help to make compost.
• Compost should have a crumbly texture.

HAVE A GO

Instead of putting your potato peelings in the compost, make a tasty and nutritious soup from them instead! You can find simple recipes on the Internet, but you may need some extra ingredients, such as onion, carrot or herbs to make it even tastier. Always ask an adult to help you with any chopping and cooking.

Make this

Recycling waste food into compost saves energy and helps the environment. Make a fun caddy to store your kitchen scraps.

Your hungry caddy will gobble up all your food scraps and help you take the waste to your compost bin.

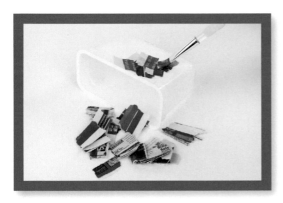

1 Tear up pieces of newspaper. Using glue and a brush, paste the pieces all over an empty, clean plastic box and lid. (A large ice cream tub is ideal.) Leave to dry.

2 Paint the outside of the box and lid green. Leave to dry.

3 Draw an eye dot on each paper or polystyrene ball with a felt-tip pen. Then paint the back half of each ball green. Leave to dry.

4 Glue the eyes on top of the lid. Cut out five triangles of white paper or card and stick them under the lid to make teeth.

GLOSSARY

atmosphere the gases that surround a planet

bacteria micro-organisms. Some bacteria are useful, some can cause diseases

biodegradable material that breaks down naturally

decompose to rot or break down

digesting breaking down food inside a body to get nutrients and energy

energy power needed to make things work

fibres threads of material

flexible bendy

furnace giant industrial oven that gets very hot

global warming the gradual warming up of the Earth's surface

goods things that are bought and sold

greenhouse gas gases such as carbon dioxide that help trap heat in the Earth's atmosphere

habitat the natural home of an animal or plant

incinerator giant oven for burning waste

iron ore rocks that we can get iron from

landfill a large hole in the ground where rubbish is buried

lime a white substance found in limestone that can corrode things

magnet an object that attracts items that contain iron, cobalt or nickel, such as steel

methane a natural gas produced when things rot

micro-organism tiny living thing people can only see with the help of a microscope

mine a place where raw materials, such as iron ore, sand or coal are dug out of the ground

mining digging raw materials out of the ground

natural found in nature

nutrients substances that living things need to help them live and grow

pollute to make something unclean or unsafe to use

polyester synthetic material, often used to make textiles

raw materials basic natural material that we can make other things from

reduce to make smaller

soda ash material used to make glass

synthetic material made using chemicals

weave to lace threads or other materials together to make sheets of textiles

BOOKS

Eco Alert: Waste and Recycling
by Rebecca Hunter (Franklin Watts , 2012)

Go Green: Reduce, Reuse, Recycle
by Helen Lanz (Franklin Watts, 2012)

Making a Difference: **(series)**
by Sue Barraclough (Franklin Watts, 2011)

Materials That Matter: **(series)**
by Neil Morris (Franklin Watts, 2011)

What Happens When We Recycle: **(series)** by Jillian Powell
(Franklin Watts, 2014)

WEBSITES

zone.recycledevon.org/games
This colourful website has information, games and activities all about the 3Rs – reducing, reusing and recycling.

www.olliesworld.com/uk/html/ explore.html
Join Ollie and his dog Buster as they discover more about reusing and recycling and take part in some fun quizzes. It also has great ideas for things you can do at home.

www.schoolsrecycle.planetark.org/ documents/doc-674-recycled-arts-and- crafts-guide.pdf
A downloadable PDF of recycling activities.

NOTE TO PARENTS AND TEACHERS:
Every effort has been made by the Publishers to ensure that these websites are suitable for children, that they are of the highest educational value, and that they contain no inappropriate or offensive material. However, because of the nature of the Internet, it is impossible to guarantee that the contents of these sites will not be altered. We strongly advise that Internet access is supervised by a responsible adult.

INDEX

QUIZ ANSWERS

Page 8: b – deforestation
Page 12: a – glass keeps its colour when it is recycled
Page 16: b – 3 hours
Page 18: c – around 500 years, but this depends on how big the bottle is
Page 24: c – fertilisers
Page 26: they are all correct answers!